Mrs. R. Sibley

D1079092

Sticky HISTORY BOOKS

EGYPTIANS

PYRAMIDS AND MOULDY MUMMIES

Written by Rosemary Border
Illustrated by Peter Rutherford and Peter Wilks

If you haven't found history a barrel of laughs so far, it's probably because you got bogged down in the boring parts. History is like a kipper - you sometimes have to work hard to get at the tasty bits. Our old history master, Mr. Salmon - inevitably nicknamed Old Fishface - was a good historian. He also knew a lot about kids; and that was what made him a good teacher. At the start of a lesson Old Fishface dished out fact sheets.

"If you learn this by heart you'll know enough about Ancient Egypt" (or castles, or the Romans, or whatever) "to pass your exams. Now I'll tell you something *really* interesting." And he did. He told us all the tasty bits.

Sometimes we were so enthralled by his tales that we didn't even hear the bell at the end of the lesson. I have forgotten almost everything in Old Fishface's fact sheets, but I can remember all his stories. I keep them in a compartment of my mind labelled Useless Information.

Sticky History is like that - real history (I didn't make any of it up, honestly!) with all the boring bits taken out. A sort of fillet of history - no skin, no bones, just the tasty bits.

Rosemary Border 1995

We know a lot more about the ancient Egyptians than we do, for example, about the ancient Britons. There are three reasons for this.

SURVIVAL KITS

First, the ancient Egyptians believed in an afterlife. Your life in this world was Stage One. After Stage One ended, you went to the underworld, where the gods weighed your heart in a pair of scales. If your soul was OK, off you trotted to the next world.

Beliefs like that are not unusual. Many religions teach people to believe in an afterlife. Many religions also preach "You can't take it with you when you go". The Egyptians, however, believed you could, and should, take it with you. They buried their dead with a complete survival kit for the afterlife. By studying these survival kits, we can learn a lot about everyday life in ancient Egypt.

HOT AND DRY

Third, Egypt is a hot, dry country (you've seen the postcards). Things that were buried there did not rot as they would have done in a damper climate. Provided nobody meddled with your grave (see Grave Robbers), there was a good chance of everything lasting, just as it was, for thousands of years.

THE WRITTEN WORD

Second, the Egyptians did heaps of writing. They simply couldn't help themselves; scribble here, scribble there. They'd paint and carve on walls. These were your original graffiti artists!

3

PHARAOH FAX

Right, here's the bit Old Fishface would have put onto a fact sheet. This is much more fun!

THE STORY OF EGYPT

About 5000 years ago, a warlike king called Menes from Upper Egypt beat up his neighbours (mean old Menes) in Lower Egypt and built a city called Memphis on the Nile (not to be confused with Elvis' Memphis, on the Mississippi). He (Menes, not Elvis) was the first Pharaoh. Memphis is where the first of the great pyramids, the Step Pyramid, was built 400 years later. Pyramids were in fashion for another 400 years. This time is called the Old Kingdom.

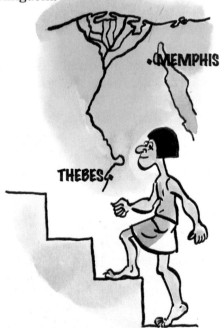

The Old Kingdom ended when the Egyptian nobles got stroppy and chose a king of their own. For a long time there were two Pharaohs, one in the north and one in the south.

At last a new family from Thebes brought the country together. This peaceful time is called the Middle Kingdom. This is the time when the best writing, art and engineering went on. But after 250 years of peace, Egypt was split again. Invaders, whom the Egyptians called the Hyksos, saw their chance and conquered Lower Egypt. The showoffs brought chariots with them, too. Before then the Egyptians didn't have a clue about the wheel. They soon made up for lost time and built chariots of their own and drove the Hyksos out. The New Kingdom began.

4

During this time Egypt had many kings and just one queen - her name was Hatshepsut, but we won't hold that against her. During the New Kingdom, Egypt became a great fighting nation. Tutankhamun, whose tomb is the most famous of all, ruled during this period.

Egypt's enemies grew stronger and bolder. More and more invaded Egypt. Just in the nick of time, a Greek (Alexander the Great) rallied round and invaded Egypt to defeat the pesky Persians. (The Greeks hated the Persians and wanted to squash them, too.) One of Alexander's generals, Ptolemy, became Pharaoh. So the next Pharaohs were not Egyptian at all, but Greek. The Ptolemys ruled Egypt for another 300 years. The last of the Ptolemys was Queen Cleopatra. The Romans invaded Egypt and she killed herself. Egypt became part of the Roman Empire.

The story of ancient Egypt was a long one - over 3,000 years - but now it was over.

OLD KINGDOM

MIDDLE KINGDOM

NEW KINGDOM

THREE THINGS EVERYONE KNOWS ABOUT CLEOPATRA!

I asked for an aspirin!

- She smuggled herself in to see the Roman general, Julius Caesar, rolled in a carpet.
- She bathed in asses' milk to keep her skin soft and smooth.
- She killed herself by letting a poisonous snake, called an asp, bite her.

There have been many stories, plays and films about her, but her true story is just as exciting.

PAPYRUS

We get our word 'paper' from 'papyrus', the reed which the Egyptians used to make their paper. It is quite different from parchment, which was made from the skins of animals.

The ancient Egyptians cornered the market in writing materials. There was a tax on it, a bit like VAT nowadays, and they sold a lot of papyrus abroad. Most of the great works of the ancient Greeks (read our Sticky History and learn all about the Trojan Horse!) were written on Egyptian papyrus.

Papyrus reeds grew - and still grow - by the River Nile, and if you mowed down a few, there were always plenty more. Papyrus was made from the pith of these reeds. Modern paper is made mainly from wood pulp - trees that have been shredded and soaked until really soggy.

D.I.Y. PAPYRUS

1 Cut your reeds from the river bank.

2 Peel away the green outside. (You can make some splendid table mats from this.)

3 Slice the white pith lengthways into wafer-thin strips.

4 Lay one layer of strips on top of another. Layer 1 goes left to right, layer 2 top to bottom (rather similar to your table mat).

5 Pound the pith into sheets with a wooden hammer.

6 Polish your papyrus with a stone to make it smooth.

Papyrus was pretty useful stuff all round. You could make boats from papyrus reeds, too. There are pyramids in Mexico, on the other side of the world. Some people believe this proves that the ancient Egyptians travelled across the Atlantic Ocean in their papyrus boats and took the secret of building pyramids with them. Well, maybe they did, but I'm not too sure. A papyrus boat was fine on the River Nile, but a big wave would do it no good at all.

POTTY TRAINING

PEN AND INK

The Egyptians wrote with reeds from the river Nile (you see how useful the river was?). Children did not use papyrus because it was too expensive. They learned to write on pieces of broken pot. Could this be potty training?

USELESS INFORMATION - SEAWORTHY?

The famous explorer Thor Heyerdahl tried crossing the Atlantic in a papyrus boat. He studied pictures and models from tombs and ordered an exact copy. The boat was called Ra, after the ancient Egyptian sun god, and it travelled thousands of miles before it became so soggy that the explorers had to abandon ship.

ONE WAY TRIP

The Egyptians believed in an afterlife, but they did not leave anything to chance. Life in the next world, the Egyptians believed, would be very like life in this one, and you would need the same things. If you arrived without your toothbrush, your make-up or your packed lunch, you would lose out. So the dead person was buried with a complete survival kit - food, furniture, spears, slaves - to use in the next world.

Some children's graves contain toys for them to play with in the next world. There are balls and tops, skittles and dolls, board games and toy animals.

toothbrush
Slaves
food

8

SLAVES IN HEAVEN

In the earliest times, when a rich person died, slaves were killed, and buried with their master or mistress so they could carry on their job in the afterlife. This was not popular with anyone, least of all the slaves who were about to be put to death. The dead person's family weren't best pleased either. Suppose your dad died. Imagine having to find a new cook, and teach her how to make perfect goat stew, just because the old cook had been buried with your old man.

One day, to everyone's great relief, someone hit on the idea of burying *models* of the real thing. These were called shabti, and they were made with tools in their hands so they could start work straight away on the 'other side'.

In the same way, while kings and queens were buried with real boats to carry their souls to heaven, lesser people had model boats instead.

9

RED AND BLACK LAND
(EGYPT, FOR SHORT)

Imagine a desert, which the ancient Egyptians called Dashre (the Red Land) with a monstrous great river (the Nile) running through the middle. That's Egypt.

Every year the Nile flooded. Whoosh! The bad thing about this was that until they learned *not* to build their homes within reach of the flooding, a lot of people had some mopping-up to do ever year. The good news was that when the flood waters drew back, they left rich soil behind, as black as liquorice. The word for this kind of soil is silt, and it is full of all the things the river has picked up on its travels. You can grow two or even three crops a year in it. The Egyptians called this fertile country Keme, the Black Land.

Bit by bit, the Egyptians reclaimed more land from the desert . They did this by digging little canals to bring the river water from the Nile to their fields far away from the river. This was irrigation. Water meant the difference between life and death - no water meant no crops and no food.

USELESS INFORMATION - TO THE POWER OF OX

The Ancient Egyptians did not use horses to work the land, because the king swiped all the horses for his army. Ever adaptable, the farmers used oxen to plough the land and to pull carts.

RED IS BAD

The bad news? Well, sometimes there was a piddling little flood, which meant a poor harvest and a lot of people going hungry. And sometimes there was a huge flood, and a lot of people near the river lost their homes.

But on the whole the Nile was good news for everyone. Without it, Egypt would be all desert. Where the water stopped, the Red Land began. Nobody lived there except wild animals and even wilder tribesmen. The Egyptians called these tribesmen the Sand People and were rarely on speaking terms with them. The Egyptians went into the Red Land to grab gold, salt and precious stones. They also buried their dead people there, away from the land of the living.

WELL PRESERVED

If the Egyptians had buried their dead in the Black Land by the river, all the evidence would have been washed away by the floods, or dug up by farmers, thousands of years ago. In the desert, the hot dry sand kept everything in good condition. Although grave robbers plundered some of the tombs, archaeologists were able to dig up a big chunk of the past from this land. (Fortunately, nobody had dug it up with heavy machines, to build multi-storey car parks or supermarkets.)

WHAT'S ON AT THE TEMPLE?

That's how we know so much about the ancient Egyptians. They built to last, and nobody bothered to knock down their buildings. So we know, for example, what life was like for the priests in a temple.

A temple was more like a small town than a church. It had its own workshops, granaries for storing corn, library and even a school. The farmland around belonged to the temple, too. The outer parts of the temple were open to everyone. People came to offer prayers to the gods. Sometimes they brought votive tablets - little pottery plaques with their prayers scratched on them and a pair of ears, meaning "Please listen!".

Only priests could enter the holy place, deep inside the temple. There they kept a statue of their god in a shrine, which looked a bit like a sentry-box.

How to care for your God:

Rules for Priests

- Place in a well-lit area - next to a window is good. (Er, just kidding on that one.)
- You must wash and shave before you go into the holy place.
- Take the statue out of its shrine.
- Sprinkle water on the statue.
- Put clean clothes on it.
- Offer it food and drink (if it answers, scarper and tell the Chief Priest!)
- Put it back in the shrine.
- Leave the doors open until evening.
- As you leave, wipe away your footprints.

Mastabas, Pyramids and Tombs

As soon as you say "Egypt", most people think "pyramids". But there were other ways of playing dead.

The earliest kings were buried in flat-topped brick tombs called 'mastabas'. The goodies in their graves show they were both rich and bloodthirsty. A picture in King Narmer's tomb showed the King clubbing his enemy to death. Right royal behaviour!

Then came the Pyramids, which were built of stone. Pyramids were in fashion for 400 years. (Not surprising, this, since they took so long to build, anyway!)

The next big craze was rock tombs and funerary temples. King Tutankhamun, whose survival kit is one of the greatest treasures ever found, was buried in one of these. Really big tombs and temples, like the Pyramids, were not easily overlooked. But, once the grave robbers had stolen the valuable stuff, many smaller tombs were forgotten for thousands of years. That was how the robbers missed Tutankhamun's tomb.

How many other tombs are out there in the desert, just waiting for someone to find them?

THE EARLY PYRAMIDS

The first pyramids started as 'high-rise' mastabas, one on top of the other, like a block of flats. The first 'real' pyramid is the step pyramid at Saqqara. It was built by the architect Imhotep for King Djoser. Well, after that, pyramids became all the rage. The biggest were built at Gîza for Khufi (who *used* to be called Cheops, but that sounded too much like a piece of meat) and Khephren, who came next.

Not all pyramids are pyramid-shaped. The bent pyramid of Snofru at Dahshur has slightly curved sides. Dare to be different.

USELESS INFORMATION - WHAT'S IN A NAME?

You probably already knew that the Egyptian kings gave themselves a grand title - Pharaoh. But did you know that the word Pharaoh comes from the word for "great house"? Thought not!

15

The Great Pyramid isn't called The Great Pyramid for nothing, take a peep at these figures:

Height: 148 metres
- which makes St Paul's Cathedral in London look titchy.

Floor area: 53,059 metres
- you could *lose* St Paul's Cathedral inside here!

Cubic Capacity: 2,500,000 cubic metres
- what is the cubic capacity of your fridge at home?

Each stone weighs: 2.5 tonnes
- that's as much as 4 small cars! Heavy, man.

USELESS INFORMATION - SLAVE LABOUR?

Most people think the Pyramids were built with slave labour (and stones, obviously). They are only half right! Many of the people who built the Pyramids *were* slaves. Some, too, were prisoners who had been captured in battle. But many were farm labourers who could not work in the fields for part of the year because of the floods. (Well, could *you* plant corn in a metre of mucky water?) The Pharaoh called them to work on his building projects until the waters went down and they could till the land again. Sometimes he even paid them!

There are over 2 million stones in the Great Pyramid - which means the total weight of all that stone is at least a whopping 5 million tonnes.

ALL THAT TO BURY ONE KING. THERE MUST BE EASIER WAYS...?

17

HOW TO BUILD A PYRAMID

The Great Pyramid was built for Khufu (that's old Cheops again), who reigned for 23 years. That's about 8400 days. Suppose he ordered his pyramid as soon as he came to the throne. That means cutting, transporting and laying about 240 blocks of stone every single day.

The ground at the base of the pyramid had to be levelled. Then ramps were built to drag the stones up, ready for each stage of the building. Each stone weighed about 2.5 tonnes and had to be transported either by land or by boat from the quarry where it was cut. Gangs of workmen and oxen dragged the stones on sledges or on rollers. They used ropes and simple bronze and stone tools - there were no power drills or clever lifting gear in those days.

They built the core of the pyramid first, then put on the outer facing, starting at the top and working down. The ramps were gradually taken down as each section was finished.

The outside of the Great Pyramid was fine white limestone, with a golden mini pyramid, called a capstone, on top. Inside were several rooms for the Pharaoh and his queen to use in the afterlife. Archaeologists found a wooden boat next to his tomb. This was probably used to carry the Pharaoh's body to its last resting place.

D.I.Y. PYRAMIDS

1 CUT THE STONE BLOCKS

a Choose a likely piece of rock.

b Cut notches and hammer wooden wedges into the notches.

c Pour water on the wedges.

d When the wood swells, it'll break the rock off cleanly.
This is where we get the saying
"It's the thin end of the wedge".

2 LEVEL THE GROUND

To make sure the site is level, dig channels and fill them with water. (Modern engineers would use a spirit level which is not nearly as much hard work.).

3 MOVE THE STONES

Easier said than done. Put tree trunks under the stone and roll it along on those. Keep taking tree trunks from behind the stone and laying them in front. That way, the stone won't roll back.

19

MUMMIES

Everybody knows that a dead body which has been preserved in the way the ancient Egyptians did, is called a mummy. Absolutely nothing to do with mothers; it may come from the French word 'momie'. Mummification was a very good way of keeping a body in good condition (and then came exercise). There are thousands of mummies in museums and private collections all over the world. Which goes to show how successful the Egyptians were at preserving their dead.

Some bodies mummify naturally if the conditions are right. Today, builders sometimes find mummified cats in the roof timbers of old buildings.

By dissecting mummies (cutting 'em up!) modern scientists can learn a lot about the diseases people suffered from. Maybe someday, someone will take DNA from a mummy and we shall have a sort of ancient Egyptian Jurassic Park...

Take two mummies, drink plenty of fluid and come and see me again in the morning.

USELESS INFORMATION - MUMMIES, MAGIC & MEDICINE

In the Middle Ages, doctors and magicians used mummies, ground up, for medicine and in magic spells.

THE KA AND THE BA

The Egyptians believed that everyone had two spirits. The *ka* was the life force and it stayed in the tomb with the body and took care of it. The *ba* was the dead person's own personality. The ancient Egyptians imagined it as a bird with a human face. The ba visited the world of the living in the daytime and came back to the tomb at night. These spirits could not survive unless the body was in good condition. In the earliest days this was no problem; the dead were buried in the sand, which dried out the body before it had time to rot. When the Egyptians started building tombs, they found the bodies rotted. This struck them as Not Quite So Groovy, because if the body rotted, the ka and the ba would pack their bags and leave home.

So they worked out a way of embalming the body to stop it from decomposing. The embalmers' workshops were on the west bank of the River Nile. You may think from all of this the Egyptians were a gloomy mob who thought about death all the time. Or, they may have enjoyed life *so* much that they wanted everyone to carry on having fun in the next world. Everyone except the slaves, that is.

D.I.Y. Mummy (DON'T READ THIS

1 Take 1 dead body. Lay it on a high table, so you don't get backache bending over it.

2 Wash it well.

3 Shave off the body hair. You can leave the hair on the head if you like.

4 Make a cut (called an incision) in the dead person's side.

5 Hack out the heart, lungs and intestines. Empty out the intestines. This is a smelly job, but don't worry - your workshop is a long way from houses and shops. Clean out the inside of the body with special chemicals.

6 Remove the brains by poking a long, thin hook - a bit like a crochet hook - up through the nostrils and into the skull. Wiggle the hook about a bit until you loosen the brains.

7 Twist the hook and yank the brains out. This means you will not damage the face. You will damage the brain, but this does not matter. Clean out the inside of the skull with special chemicals. There must be nothing left inside the body that can rot. You can leave the eyes in place; they will dry out naturally.

8 Place the stomach, brains, lungs and intestines in special pots called Canopic jars. Seal the jars. Keep the heart separate - you will need it later.

9 Put the body in a bath of natron (a salt made up of sodium and carbon) for at least 40 days. While you're waiting for the natron, make three coffins.

10 Take the body out of the natron and wash it again.

11 Fluff out the inside of the body with linen and bags of sweet-smelling spices.

USELESS INFORMATION - HEART AND SOUL

To the ancient Egyptians, the heart was the centre of all thoughts and feelings. You could go to the next world without a stomach or brain, but your heart had to be inside your body. Could this be the origin of the old saying, "His heart's in the right place"?

14 Put a funeral mask over the face. Add jewels and amulets to taste.

13 Wrap the body with bandages coated in resin (sap from pine trees) and sweet-smelling spices.

12 Pop the heart inside the chest and stitch the body up again.

MORE ABOUT MUMMIES
AMULETS

Amulets were good luck charms to keep evil spirits away. No well-dressed mummy should be without one. Most had several, tucked inside the bandages. Tutankhamun's mummy was loaded with them. I suppose the priests thought that if one god did not protect him, another might - like holding your trousers up with belt, braces and a piece of strong string!

The **ankh**, like a cross with a ring on top, meant life.

The **scarab** was Khepri, the giant dung beetle who, the Egyptians believed, rolled the sun between his feet just as a dung beetle rolls his ball of muck.

Anubis was the god of embalmers, the people who preserved mummies. He had a jackal's head. Embalmers sometimes wore jackal heads at work. Very practical, boys.

Bes was always shown as a funny, fat little dwarf. he brought good luck and happiness in the home.

COFFINS

Every mummy also needed *three* body-shaped coffins that fitted one inside the other like Russian dolls. Each had to be painted inside and out with magic words and pictures. The mummy fitted inside the smallest coffin, then the two outer coffins went on top. This kind of coffin is called a sarcophagus (sar-coff-a-gus). As the old song says, "It wasn't the cough that carried him off, 'twas the coffin they carried him off in."

SACRED ANIMALS

The Egyptians had a whole menagerie of sacred creatures, because most of their gods took the shape of animals or birds at some time or other. Models and pictures of these sacred animals were buried with them. Then if, by any chance, one god did not protect the dead person, another would step in and do the job.

The jackal was sacred to Anubis and the ibis bird was the special pet of the god Thoth, who was supposed to help the spirit of the dead person to travel to the afterlife in safety. The keen-eyed falcon was sacred to Horus, the son of the sun god. The Egyptians often painted the Eye of Horus inside their tombs, perhaps to keep an eye on grave robbers. At Bubastis, there was a whole cemetery of mummified cats in honour of the cat goddess Bast.

Such an honour.

USELESS INFORMATION - A CROC OF GOLD

The crocodile was sacred to the god Sebek. There was a sacred crocodile in Lake Moeris which wore gold earrings and bracelets studded with jewels. Pilgrims fed him with the choicest food. If he accepted your gift, that meant good fortune. However, the greatest honour of all was to fall into the Nile and be eaten by a crocodile.

The goddess Taueret was supposed to protect women in childbirth. She was usually pictured as a pregnant hippopotamus. The goddess Hathor, whose animal was the cow, protected women, especially when they were doing their hair or putting on their make-up. Many Egyptian mirrors have Hathor's horns and ears in her honour.

A Big Funeral

Let's eavesdrop on the funeral of an important man. His body has been with the embalmers for a month or more, so his family have had plenty of time to get everything ready. He probably ordered his tomb several years ago, and chose all the paintings and the survival kit to go inside.

On the day of the funeral, the family fetch the mummy (Daddy's mummy, in this case) and put it in a box decorated with flowers. They put the box in a boat-shaped cart pulled by oxen. The boat is in honour of the sun god Ra. Every day, the Egyptians believe, Ra travels across the sky in his golden boat. The idea of a funeral boat is to help the dead person to go and meet Ra in the afterlife.

The priest walks in front, waving an incense burner about and sprinkling milk on the ground. Behind the 'boat' comes a sort of sledge with the Canopic jars (with dead bloke's stomach, intestines, brains and lungs).

Enter stage left the professional mourners, dressed in blue. Blue, not black, remember, was the colour of sadness and death in ancient Egypt. The mourners are crying and screaming, smearing their faces with dirt and tearing their hair and their clothes. Of course the dead person's family and friends cry, too, but the professional mourners put them to shame. They are well paid to cry, and they give good value for money!

Next in line are men in kilts and tall white headdresses, dancing and clapping their hands above their heads.

There is a long procession of slaves with the grave goods - the survival kit to be put in the tomb. Thankfully, the slaves themselves do not have to die. Shabti figures will be buried in their place. So, the slaves look quite happy as they carry furniture, food, lamps and musical instruments and board games.

29

"I CAN SEE CLEARLY NOW..."

As soon as family, friends and perfect strangers have gathered at the tomb, the priest has to perform a ceremony called the Opening of the Mouth. This is supposed to give the mummy back its five senses - sight, hearing, touch and so on - ready for the next life. They prop the mummy up inside the tomb and the priest touches the mummy's mouth with a special tool like the one a carpenter used to smooth wood. While he is doing this, he says some magic words.

Now the mummy is popped inside its nest of coffins, and a copy of the Book of the Dead is put in beside it. The Book of the Dead is a list of over 200 spells to help the dead man through the dark and dangerous underworld and into Heaven. A little light reading for the journey.

Once the mummy and all the grave goods have been put inside, the tomb can be sealed and the family and friends can all go home for the funeral feast.

THE BOOK OF THE DEAD

The picture below is adapted from The Book of the Dead, and shows the heart of a dead person being weighed. The heart is in one pan of the scales and the Feather of Truth is in the other. The two have to balance exactly. If they do, the dead person is innocent and the god Osiris will welcome him to Paradise. He will even give him a wife to keep him company.

If the dead man is guilty, the monster beside the scales, whose name is Ammut, will get a free meal. Ammut is not an attractive proposition. He is the Devourer: he is part lion, part crocodile, part hippopotamus (eh?). If the dead man is guilty, Ammut will open his crocodile jaws and gobble up his heart. And without his heart, the dead man will never get to Heaven.

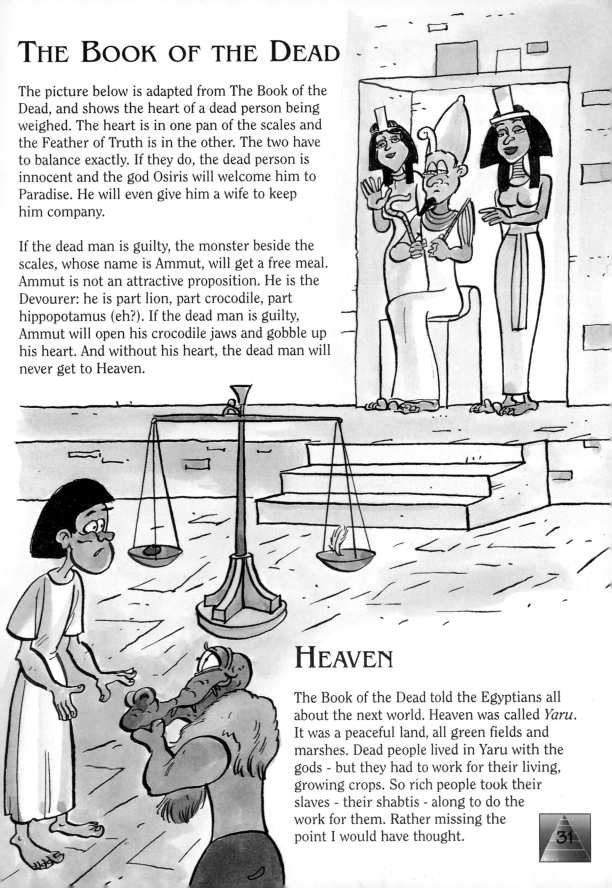

HEAVEN

The Book of the Dead told the Egyptians all about the next world. Heaven was called *Yaru*. It was a peaceful land, all green fields and marshes. Dead people lived in Yaru with the gods - but they had to work for their living, growing crops. So rich people took their slaves - their shabtis - along to do the work for them. Rather missing the point I would have thought.

GRAVE ROBBERS

Many ancient Egyptian tombs were looted almost as soon as they were built. Grave robbers came at dead of night (no daylight robbery in those days) with tools to break into the burial chambers and sacks to carry away their loot. You couldn't keep a big funeral a secret. You had to bury a full survival kit: the more important the person, the more costly the kit, and the robbers knew all about that.

There was a lot of it about - even the priests did a spot of grave-robbing. There is a painted papyrus in the British Museum which tells how the funerary temple of the Pharaoh Rameses II was robbed by its own priests. So who could you trust?

Gold was valuable stuff and most customers did not care where it came from. Some ancient grave robbers were caught and brought to justice. We know, because there is a papyrus which describes their trial in 1126 BC! But many grave robbers got away with it. How would you guard a tomb full of treasure in a lonely place, 24 hours a day?

Page 2

Page 2

Page 3

Page 2

Page 5

Page 9

Page 5

Page 8

Page 8

Page 8

Page 17

Page 14

Page 11

Page 17

Page 16

Page 11

Page 11

Page 11

Page 16

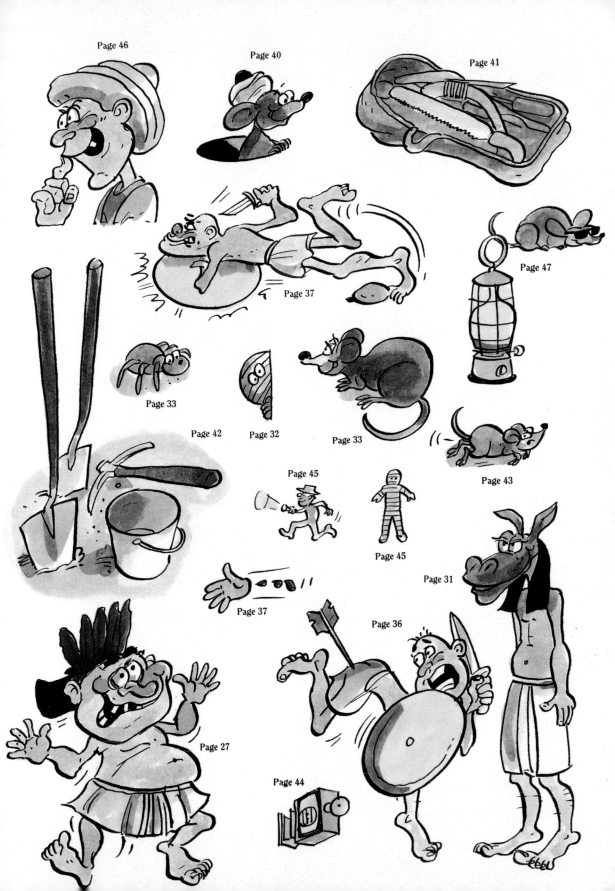

Page 46

Page 40

Page 41

Page 37

Page 47

Page 33

Page 42

Page 32

Page 33

Page 43

Page 45

Page 45

Page 31

Page 37

Page 36

Page 27

Page 44

Page 10

Page 22

Page 23

Page 23

Page 22

Page 23

Page 23

Page 23

Page 34

Page 35

Page 23

Page 28

Page 35

Page 28

Page 29

Page 28

BOOK OF SPELLS

Page 30

Page 18

Page 19

Page 26

Page 20

Page 21

Page 12

Page 20

Page 4

Page 33

Page 5

Page 13

Page 12

Page 7

Page 21

Page 6

Page 6

Page 7

At the funeral ceremony, the priests cast spells which were supposed to keep grave robbers away (unless, of course, the grave robber was the priest...). Although there are stories about the Curse of the Mummy's Tomb even today, the spells did not seem to stop the grave robbers. A lot of the gold that was placed in tombs found its way back to the workshops and into new tombs. Luckily, the early robbers left many other things untouched, items less costly but more interesting than gold and jewels.

I BET YOU DIDN'T KNOW...

... that robbers got to Tutankhamun's survival kit thousands of years before the archaeologists did. They started rummaging through the furniture, chariots and so on even before the Pharaoh's funeral! But they must have been disturbed before they could carry off their loot, because the stuff was left there, all higgledy-piggledy in the room next to the burial chamber, until Howard Carter, the famous archaeologist, found it.

THE NEW GRAVE ROBBERS

As time went by, customs changed, and the shifting sand buried the smaller monuments. People no longer remembered what the big monuments, like the pyramids, were for. The secrets of ancient Egypt were forgotten for thousands of years.Then, around 1500 AD, people became interested in the ancient world and travellers brought home mummies and amulets. These souvenirs fascinated people in Western Europe.and America. They began to delve into Egypt's past, trying to discover her secrets from the treasures.

A PRESENT FROM THEBES...

In the 18th century, people began to go on the Grand Tour - a long trip abroad to learn about other countries, languages and ways of life. Egypt became one of *the* places to visit, and no Grand Tour was complete without a few souvenirs of ancient Egypt. The tourists did not understand much about the people who lived there long ago, but it was nice to bring home a statuette or an amulet to bore your friends with at dinner parties. Grave robbers worked hard to keep them supplied.

When the French general Napoleon invaded Egypt in 1798, he took 200 learned men with him to explore and describe the country. And grave robbing became really big business again.

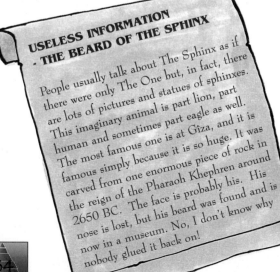

USELESS INFORMATION - THE BEARD OF THE SPHINX

People usually talk about The Sphinx as if there were only The One but, in fact, there are lots of pictures and statues of sphinxes. This imaginary animal is part lion, part human and sometimes part eagle as well. The most famous one is at Gîza, and it is famous simply because it is so huge. It was carved from one enormous piece of rock in the reign of the Pharaoh Khephren around 2650 BC. The face is probably his. His nose is lost, but his beard was found and is now in a museum. No, I don't know why nobody glued it back on!

THE ROBBERS' HOARD

In 1871 the Abdelrassoul family found a collection of mummies and grave goods in a rock tunnel. It was like winning the pools. They kept their find a deathly secret. For 10 years they stole things out of it and sold them to dealers. They used the tomb like a bank: they took things out as and when they needed money.

When at last the robbers' secret hoard was discovered, 36 royal mummies and about 6000 objects were found. The amazing thing is that ancient Egyptian court officials had moved these mummies from their original graves 3000 years earlier to save them from earlier grave robbers.

... AND ARCHAEOLOGISTS

The difference between a grave robber and an archaeologist is that a grave robber is only looking for something he can sell. Ancient grave robbers stuck to gold and jewels.

Later grave robbers started out taking only 'valuables'. Later, when they found that museums wanted other things, too, they stole those; but they were not interested in them except as a way of making money. Archaeologists are not interested in valuables, except as part of the whole picture of what life was like in ancient times. To them, a small piece of papyrus may be as important as a solid gold coffin.

THE EGYPTIANS AT WAR

We often forget that there was more to life in ancient Egypt than tombs. Egypt had some stroppy neighbours, so her people had to learn about fighting. They copied chariots from their old enemies the Hyksos, who came from the east and for a long time threatened to take over Egypt altogether. The Egyptians got their heads around the 'chariot' idea so well that they booted the horrible Hyksos out.

There was no full-time army in Egypt. Egyptian soldiers worked in the fields in peacetime, and had to be called up to go to war. They all queued up to be given their weapons and to hear the Pharaoh's pep talk .

A soldier's life was not an easy one. But he hoped that if he fought bravely - and if he didn't get killed - the Pharaoh would reward him with land to farm, and maybe some foreign prisoners to work on the land as slaves.

3 SURE-FIRE WAYS TO WIN A BATTLE

1 Make sure you have plenty of chariots, each with two men. One man controls the horses while the other shoots arrows into the enemy or stabs at them with a spear.

2 Have plenty of archers on foot, each with his quiver of arrows at his side. They shoot a rain of arrows to soften up the enemy before the foot soldiers move in.

3 Now bring in your foot soldiers, each with his long spear or axe. The foot soldiers should have shields to protect them from enemy weapons.

36

WHEN YOU'VE WON...

And, let's face it, you're going to with those battle tactics. You need to count the dead bodies to tell the Pharaoh how well you've done. There is a very easy way of doing this. Cut the hands off each stiff and pile the hands up neatly, 100 to each pile. It is quicker to count hands than whole bodies. You can bury the dead if you have time, or you can let the jackals and vultures have a free feast.

Waste not, want not! Strip the clothes off the bodies and collect their weapons. You can burn anything that isn't any use to you.

Take plenty of prisoners. You can sell them as slaves. Chain them together by their necks and march them away in a long line. That way, one man can control 20 or more slaves.

Can I give you a hand?

THE RIDDLE OF EGYPTIAN WRITING

At first nobody could read the ancient Egyptians' writing (do you have that problem, too?). Then in 1799, at Rosetta in Egypt, some French soldiers found a stone with writing in ancient Egyptian, later Egyptian (Coptic) and ancient Greek. The Rosetta Stone is now in the British Museum in London. A clever French scholar called Champollion started work on it. He knew Greek and Coptic, and he spotted the name of a king, Ptolemy, and a queen, Cleopatra (Kliopadra). It was 14 years before he understood even one word of the Egyptian language. And it took him over 20 years to read the whole message. But he kept on trying, and at last he cracked the code. Then archaeologists could at last read the thousands of inscriptions the ancient Egyptians had left behind them.

WRITE LIKE AN EGYPTIAN...

The Egyptians had two kinds of writing, hieratic and hieroglyphic. Hieratic writing was a kind of shorthand, and was used for business. It was a little like our handwriting - everyone had his or her own style. It was quick and easy to write. Very few people's handwriting is as clear and regular as print in a book, but it is fine for everyday use. Hieratic writing was like that.

Hieroglyphic writing was the 'official' writing which was used on monuments and in important documents. It had to be done very carefully and neatly. It had thousands of hieroglyphs - picture signs - and the scribes, whose job it was to write and carve the hieroglyphs had to study hard to learn them all. They studied at the Temple, in a place called the House of Life where all the papyrus scrolls were kept. It was rather like a cross between a university and a library. Each sign meant something. An ox meant an ox (what else?). A pair of walking legs meant "Go".

As time went on, instead of having a picture of an ox to mean "ox", the Egyptians started to use signs to show sounds - like our ABC. So they could put several signs together to make a word, just as we write P - O - T to mean a pot.

Here is the ABC
in ancient Egyptian.
You never know when
it'll come in handy.

K L I O P A D R A

a

i (ee)

i (ai)

a

w

b

p

f

m

n

r

h

kh

kh

h

both = S

b

k

g

39

THE VALLEY OF THE KINGS

By about 1500 BC all the pyramids had been looted. They had been enormously slow and expensive to build, and useless against grave robbers.

The later Pharaohs built hidden tombs in the rock in what we now call the Valley of the Kings. (The Valley of the Queens, in case you ask, is close by.)

Imagine a temple which led to a tunnel cut into a rocky cliff, with several beautifully decorated halls and a burial chamber deep inside. You didn't need to be royal to be buried here, and some of the non-royal tombs have the most interesting wall paintings which tell us a lot about everyday life in ancient Egypt. But sadly, the grave robbers got there first...

USELESS INFORMATION - EXCUSES, EXCUSES!

Many messages have been found, written on pieces of pottery because papyrus was expensive, about the workmen who built the tombs. There are even lists of workmen, and of the food that was bought to feed them.

These workmen were not slaves or prisoners of war; they were skilled craftsmen who were paid wages. They worked for ten days, then sloped off to their village for a break. They were often lazy, slow or late, and they had plenty of excuses. One had to "take a sick donkey to the vet". Another took time off three times in one year to bury the same dead aunt. The first recorded strike took place when the workers downed tools because food supplies were late.

THE WORK FORCE

Gangs of workers laboured for years to build these tombs. It wasn't such a huge job as building the Pyramids, but it still took a lot of men and materials. The men did not go home after work each night, because it was too far to travel. So they lived in special villages. They had wives and children there, and the children went to school. We know, because their work has been found, marked in red ink by their teacher!

Archaeologists have found these villages where the people lived who built the tombs in the Valley of the Kings. These villages weren't shanty-towns; they were in use for 300 years! After the workmen left, the sand and the dry desert air kept the buildings in good condition.

"WONDERFUL THINGS!"

On 3 November 1922 the archaeologist Howard Carter found a step buried in the sand. That sounds like the beginning of an adventure story, but really it is almost the end of a long story.

Carter worked for Lord Carnarvon, a rich Englishman who was interested in history in general and ancient Egypt in particular. Lord Carnarvon and Carter excavated (dug) together in Egypt for several years until the First World War came and Carnarvon had to go back to England. Carter stayed on, and very carefully, he excavated the Valley of the Kings.

He had a gang of Egyptian workmen who were paid with his boss's money. He taught them how to dig without destroying any evidence. He made careful notes of everything he found, comparing each tomb with what he knew about the history of Egypt. He really deserved to find something exciting, and he did - but only just in time. Lord Carnarvon was getting impatient, and Carter had a hard job persuading him to pay for just one more season's digging...

When his workmen found the step, which led to a walled-up doorway, Carter sent a telegram to his boss. Lord Carnarvon hurried to Egypt. He and Carter watched while workmen uncovered a passageway. The passageway led to a bricked-up doorway. Carter made a hole, and held a candle up to it.

"Can you see anything?" called Lord Carnarvon anxiously.

"Yes," replied Carter. "Wonderful things!"

They had found the tomb of the Pharaoh Tutankhamun.

USELESS INFORMATION - CURSE OR COINCIDENCE?

There have been many stories about the Curse of the Mummy's Tomb. According to legend, everyone connected with the discovery of Tutankhamun's tomb died suddenly and painfully.

Lord Carnarvon was bitten by a mosquito soon after finding Tutankhamun's tomb. The bite got infected and he died in March 1923. The story goes that back in Britain, at the exact moment of his death, his dog howled and died. At the same moment the electricity supply failed in Cairo and all the lights went out. Meanwhile, two other people connected with the tomb had died... wow - what a story!

...Except that Howard Carter did not die until 1939. And most of the other archaeologists who worked on Tutankhamun's tomb lived to a ripe old age.

43

TREASURES OF TUTANKHAMUN

Tutankhamun's tomb was the only Egyptian tomb ever to be found complete. In the first room was the Pharaoh's survival kit: beds, chairs, chests, chariots, clothes and food for his long journey to the next world. They were all thrown together like junk in a jumble sale. As Carter examined everything, he realised that thieves had been there before him. They had disturbed the grave goods (serious stuff), but something had happened to stop them from getting away with them. What had happened? Did someone catch the thieves red-handed and punish them? Or was it a one of those spells the priests cast when old Tootie was buried originally? Oo-er. We shall never know.

HUNT THE MUMMY

Getting to the body of the Pharaoh was like a game of Pass the Parcel. By the time you get your prize the floor is littered with wrapping paper. Tutankhamun's tomb was just like that.

Inside the innermost room of the tomb there was a golden shrine - a sort of mini-temple for a god. Inside that was another shrine, and another, and another - four shrines altogether. The seals on the doors of the first shrine were broken, and on the floor nearby were things which the thieves, in their hurry, must have dropped.

The second shrine was intact. So was the third. Then came the fourth, and the sarcophagus saw the light of day for the first time in thousands of years.

THE THREE COFFINS

The sarcophagus was made of red sandstone. Each corner was carved with a beautiful winged goddess. But the lid was smashed in two pieces. What had been happening?

Inside the sarcophagus were the Pharaoh's three mummy-shaped coffins. A wreath of flowers lay on the first coffin. It was made of gilded wood, wrapped in linen, and it represented Osiris, the God of the Dead. Handy god to have around, under the circumstances.

Inside the first coffin was the second coffin. It was gilded wood, too, but inlaid all over with flowers made of many-coloured glass. On it lay a great sheaf of olive and willow leaves and blue lotus flowers. To the Egyptians the lotus was a magic flower.

The third coffin was not just gilded wood. It was made of solid gold. A necklace of flowers lay on it. The coffin was decorated with figures of Nekhabet, the vulture, and Wadjet, the serpent. Inside was the mummy of the King, with a beautiful gold death mask.

TUTANKHAMUN'S MUMMY

If getting to the mummy was like Passing the Parcel, unwrapping the mummy of Tutankhamun was more like doctors whipping the bandages off an injured person to see what was going on underneath. Of course, before the experts could start work the mummy had to be taken from the tomb and put in a laboratory where the air would be just warm enough and dry enough to keep the body in good condition.

TIKKA TUTANKHAMUN

There were hundreds of metres of very fine linen. The bandages had not just been cut from a big sheet - they had been woven specially. Every part of the body was wrapped in this beautiful white linen. Each finger and toe was bandaged individually.

But the experts had a shock. Inside all these bandages, the Pharaoh's mummy was not at all well-preserved. They would unwind the bandages from a finger, and the finger would come away in their hands (from his hand)! They realised the problem almost at once. The embalmers had used too many spices. Instead of preserving the body, the spices had burned away the flesh and started attacking the bones. Perhaps the embalmers thought that if a little did a good job, a lot would be even better. They were wrong.

I think he's a bit pickled.

Gold Hold

Only the parts of the Pharaoh's body that were protected by gold were preserved. But the mummy was literally covered with treasures. Altogether there were 143 golden amulets and trinkets tucked under the bandages: finger-stalls, bracelets, sandals, necklaces, crowns, daggers, earrings...

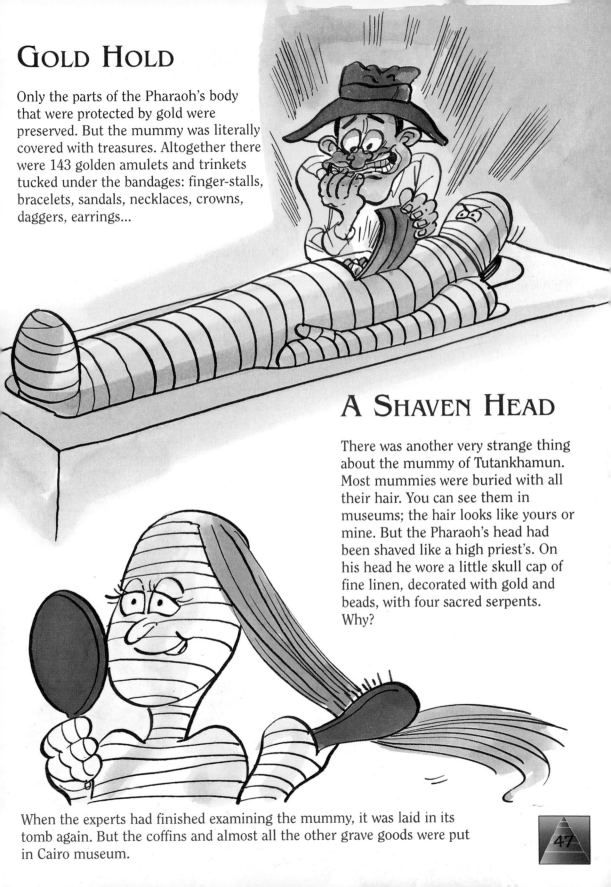

A Shaven Head

There was another very strange thing about the mummy of Tutankhamun. Most mummies were buried with all their hair. You can see them in museums; the hair looks like yours or mine. But the Pharaoh's head had been shaved like a high priest's. On his head he wore a little skull cap of fine linen, decorated with gold and beads, with four sacred serpents. Why?

When the experts had finished examining the mummy, it was laid in its tomb again. But the coffins and almost all the other grave goods were put in Cairo museum.

"TUTANKHAMUN, THIS WAS YOUR LIFE"

WHO WAS I?

You were called Tutankhaten when you were born. You changed your name when you became Pharaoh. You came to the throne when you were about 9 and died (sorry about that) when you were only about 20 years old.

WHEN DID I LIVE?

You were born about 1362 BC, came to the throne about 1351 BC and died about 1342 BC. (BC dates count backwards. It's like saying "Only four - three - two days to my birthday" or counting down before blast-off.)

WHAT DID I DIE OF?

Sorry to bring it up again, but your body was too badly damaged for anything obvious to be found. Maybe you were murdered, maybe you died of a fever. Lots of people died young in those days, if that makes you feel any better. No, I don't suppose it does.

WAS I MARRIED?

Yes, indeed. How could you forget her? Your queen was called Ankhesenamun. (There was even a picture of the two of you together on the back of your throne.)

DID I HAVE ANY CHILDREN?

Nobody knows of any. But here's a very strange thing - in your tomb two fetuses - unborn babies - were found. Each had been mummified and laid in a tiny coffin.
Were they your children? Nobody knows.

WHAT HAPPENED TO MY WIFE?

As far as we know, she died of old age.

WHAT WAS PERHAPS MY FAVOURITE THING IN ALL THESE TREASURES?

There was a wonderful board game, like a cross between chess and backgammon. It often ended in dead heats.

THE END OF THE STORY - OR IS IT?

That, as Old Fishface used to say, is all we have time for today. But it is not the end of the story. The ancient Egyptians flourished for thousands of years. Everyone died, and everyone was buried with a survival kit of some kind. Even quite ordinary people, like temple scribes or engineers, had fine tombs with rich grave goods. It is certain that only a small proportion of those have been found. What treasures are lying, still waiting to be discovered?